GOING UP?

SOFT SKILLS TO GAIN PROMOTED AT WORK

BY.... *OLUWASEGUN AINA*

© **2021 OLUWASEGUN AINA.** All rights reserved.

No part of this publication may be reproduced, distributed, or transmitted in any form or by any means, including photocopying, recording, or other electronic or mechanical methods, without the prior written permission of the Author. For permission requests, contacthinklet@gmail.com

The story, all names, characters, and incidents portrayed in this book are fictitious. No identification with actual persons (living or deceased), places, buildings, and products is intended or should be inferred.

Book Cover by **Oluwasegun Aina**

DEDICATION

This book is dedicated to the glory of God.

TABLE OF CONTENT

Introduction

Chapter 1
◆ Understanding yourself ……..p8
◆ Employee promotion ……. p10
◆ Meaning of soft skills   …….p14

Chapter 2 (soft skills)
1. Communication ………….. 17
2. Relationship building ……..24
3. Positive attitude …………….32
4. Work ethic ……………………39
5. Persuasion skill ……………..47
6. Negotiation skill …………….54
7. Teamwork …………………….61
8. Emotional intelligence……..69
9. Empathy ……………………….81
10. Time management ………..87
11. Problem -solving skill …….96
12. Adaptability ………………..104
13. Leadership skill …………..112

INTRODUCTION

Soft skills are often overlooked in the job search and promotion process, yet they can be some of the most valuable assets an employee possesses in getting what he/she wants. In this book, we will explore the various ways that developing and showcasing soft skills can lead to job promotion. From communication and collaboration to leadership and adaptability, we will delve into the importance of these intangible skills and offer practical tips for improving and showcasing them in the workplace. Whether you are looking to climb the corporate ladder or simply want to stand out in your current position, this book will provide valuable insights and strategies for leveraging your soft skills to achieve your career goals.

CHAPTER ONE

UNDERSTANDING YOURSELF

Understanding oneself is a crucial aspect of personal growth and development. It involves knowing one's strengths, weaknesses, beliefs, values, and motivations. This understanding can be achieved through self-reflection, seeking feedback from others, and learning from life experiences.

Self-reflection is the process of examining one's thoughts, feelings, and behaviors. It involves asking oneself questions such as "Why do I feel this way?" or "What motivates me to do this?" By examining our own emotions and actions, we can gain insight into our own motivations and behaviors. This can help us understand why we do certain things and how we can make better decisions in the future.

Seeking feedback from others is another way to understand oneself. By asking friends, family, or even a therapist for their perspective on our actions and behaviors, we can gain a different perspective on ourselves. This can help us identify patterns or behaviors that we may not have noticed ourselves.

Finally, learning from life experiences is an important way to understand oneself. Every experience we have shapes who we are and how we view the world. By examining our past experiences and the lessons we have learned from them, we can better understand our own beliefs, values, and motivations.

In conclusion, understanding oneself is an ongoing process that involves self-reflection, seeking feedback from others, and learning from life experiences. It is an important aspect of personal growth and development, as it allows us to make informed decisions and navigate the world with a better understanding of who we are and what we stand for.

EMPLOYEE PROMOTION

Employee promotion is the process of advancing an employee to a higher position or rank within an organization. This can be a rewarding and motivating experience for employees, as it not only allows them to take on more responsibility and challenges, but it can also come with a pay increase and other benefits. However, the process of promoting an employee is not always straightforward and can involve a variety of factors and considerations.

One of the most important considerations in the promotion process is an employee's job performance. This includes not only their job-specific skills and abilities, but also their overall contribution to the organization. An employee who consistently produces high-quality work, meets deadlines, and goes above and beyond in their duties is more likely to be considered for promotion. Additionally, an employee who has a positive attitude and good communication skills is more likely to be seen as a valuable asset to the organization.

Another important factor in employee promotion is an employee's experience and education. This includes both their work experience within the organization and any relevant education or training they may have received. An employee who has a strong track record of success within the organization and has taken the time to develop their skills and knowledge is more likely to be seen as a strong candidate for promotion.

However, it's not just an employee's individual qualities that are taken into consideration when it comes to promotion. The needs of the organization also play a role. This includes the current workload and staffing needs of the organization, as well as the overall goals and objectives of the company. An employee who is well-suited to the needs of the organization and can contribute to the achievement of its goals is more likely to be considered for promotion.

The promotion process can vary from organization to organization. Some companies have a formal process in place for promotions, while others may be more informal. In either case, it's important for employees to be proactive in seeking out opportunities for advancement. This can include seeking out new challenges and responsibilities within their current role, as well as seeking out training and development opportunities.

Employee promotion can be a complex and competitive process. However, with hard work, dedication, and a commitment to continuous learning and improvement, employees can increase their chances of success and advance their careers within their organization.

MEANING OF SOFT SKILLS

Soft skills are personal qualities and attributes that are not directly related to a person's job or technical skills, but rather their ability to interact with others and work effectively in a team. Examples of soft skills include communication, problem-solving, conflict resolution, time management, and leadership. These skills are important in any role and are often valued by employers as they can help improve productivity, foster positive relationships, and enhance overall team performance.

In this book, we shall be looking at 13 soft skills which are highly needed in every organization. These soft skills include: communication skills, relationship-building skills, positive attitude, work ethic, persuasion skills, negotiation skills, teamwork, emotional intelligence, empathy, time management, problem-solving, adaptability and leadership skills.

CHAPTER TWO
(SOFT SKILLS)

1. COMMUNICATION

Effective communication is an important skill in any workplace, and it can certainly play a role in helping you achieve promotions and other career advancements. Here are some ways that good communication can aid promotion at work:

Improved relationships with coworkers and supervisors: Strong communication skills can help you build positive relationships with your coworkers and supervisors. These relationships can be a key factor in being considered for promotions or other opportunities within the company.

Increased productivity: Good communication can help you work more efficiently and effectively with your team. This can lead to increased productivity and a better overall performance, which can be attractive to those considering you for promotions.

Enhanced problem-solving skills: Clear and effective communication can help you work through problems and come up with creative solutions. This can be especially valuable in leadership roles, where the ability to solve problems and make decisions is key.

Stronger negotiation skills: Good communication can also help you negotiate for promotions, raises, and other benefits. Being able to clearly articulate your value to the company and why you deserve a promotion can be critical in these discussions.

Improved reputation: Being a skilled communicator can help you build a strong reputation within the company, which can be beneficial when it comes to being considered for promotions or other opportunities.

Overall, good communication is an essential skill that can help you succeed in your career and achieve promotions. By developing your communication skills and using them effectively, you can increase your chances of advancement and success in the workplace.

SCENARIO...
There was a time when Mary was just a junior employee at her company, working hard day in and day out to meet the expectations of her superiors. However, deep down inside, Mary had always dreamed of rising through the ranks and becoming a leader in the organization.

One day, Mary decided that it was time to take matters into her own hands and start working towards her dream of getting a promotion. She knew that this would require a lot of hard work and dedication, but she was willing to do whatever it took to achieve her goal.

The first thing that Mary did was to focus on improving her communication skills. She realized that effective communication was the key to success in any organization, and she was determined to become the best communicator she could be.

To start with, Mary made effort to always be clear and concise when speaking to her colleagues and superiors. She avoided using jargon or technical terms that might be confusing to others, and instead chose simple and straightforward language that everyone could understand.

In addition to this, Mary also made sure to listen carefully to what others had to say, and asked clarifying questions whenever necessary. She understood that effective communication was not just about talking, but also about understanding others and being able to engage in meaningful dialogue.

As Mary continued to work on her communication skills, she began to see some positive results. Her colleagues started to trust and respect her more, and she found that she was able to build stronger relationships with them.

At the same time, Mary also made an effort to be more proactive in her work. She took on additional responsibilities and went above and beyond to complete tasks to the best of her ability. She knew that this would not only help her stand out from the crowd, but also show her superiors that she was ready for a promotion.

As the months passed, Mary's hard work and dedication started to pay off. She was recognized for her excellent communication skills and her willingness to take on extra responsibilities, and she was eventually offered a promotion to a leadership role.

Mary was overjoyed at the news, and she knew that her efforts to improve her communication skills had played a major role in her success. She was grateful to her colleagues and superiors for their support and encouragement, and she was ready to take on the new challenges that came with her new role.

Looking back, Mary realized that effective communication had been the key to her success. It had helped her to build stronger relationships with her colleagues, and it had opened up new opportunities for her within the organization. She was grateful for the chance to grow and learn, and she was excited to see what the future held for her in her new position.

2. POSITIVE ATTITUDE

Having a positive attitude at work can make a world of difference in your daily life and the lives of those around you. It can impact your productivity, your relationships with coworkers, and your overall satisfaction with your job. Here are 5000 words on the importance of maintaining a positive attitude at work:

Positive attitudes can lead to increased productivity. When you approach tasks with a positive attitude, you are more likely to see challenges as opportunities to learn and grow, rather than obstacles that stand in your way. This can lead to a greater sense of accomplishment and motivation to keep going. In contrast, negative attitudes can lead to procrastination, frustration, and lower-quality work.

Positive attitudes can also enhance your relationships with coworkers. When you approach interactions with a positive attitude, you are more likely to foster a sense of collaboration and teamwork. This can lead to better communication, greater trust, and a more enjoyable work environment for everyone. On the other hand, negative attitudes can lead to conflict, resentment, and a breakdown in communication.

Maintaining a positive attitude can also lead to greater job satisfaction. When you approach your work with a positive attitude, you are more likely to find meaning and purpose in your job. This can lead to a greater sense of accomplishment and fulfillment, which can in turn lead to greater job satisfaction. Negative attitudes, on the other hand, can lead to feelings of boredom, frustration, and a lack of fulfillment in your work.

There are several ways to maintain a positive attitude at work:

Practice gratitude - Taking time to appreciate what you have and what you have accomplished can help to shift your perspective and focus on the positive aspects of your job.

Stay positive even in difficult situations - It's natural to feel frustrated or overwhelmed at times, but try to find the silver lining in every situation. Look for ways to problem-solve and find solutions rather than dwelling on the negative.

Surround yourself with positive people - The people you spend time with can have a big impact on your attitude. Surrounding yourself with positive, supportive people can help to lift your mood and keep you motivated.

Take breaks and practice self-care - It's important to take breaks and recharge your batteries to maintain a positive attitude. This could include things like taking a walk, meditating, or engaging in activities that bring you joy.

Set achievable goals and celebrate your achievements- Setting goals can help to keep you motivated and focused, and celebrating your achievements can help to boost your confidence and positive attitude.

Practice positive self-talk -The way you talk to yourself can have a big impact on your attitude. Try to focus on the positive aspects of your job and your own abilities, and remind yourself of your successes and strengths.

Focus on the present moment- It can be easy to get caught up in the stress and negativity of the past or the future, but focusing on the present moment can help to keep you grounded and present.

Find purpose in your work- When you find meaning and purpose in your work, it can help to keep you motivated and engaged. Look for ways to make a difference in your job, whether it's through your own contributions or by helping others.

Learn from setbacks and failures- It's natural to experience setbacks and failures at work, but it's important to look at these experiences as opportunities to learn and grow. Focusing on the positive aspects of these experiences can help to maintain a positive attitude.

Seek out opportunities for personal and professional growth- When you are actively working to improve and grow, it can help to keep

SCENARIO...
As the youngest member of the marketing team at XYZ Corporation, Rachel had always been eager to prove herself and move up the ladder. She knew that hard work and dedication were important, but she also believed that having a positive attitude could make a big difference in her career.

Despite facing numerous challenges and setbacks, Rachel always tried to stay positive and look for ways to improve. She knew that a negative attitude could bring down the entire team, and she didn't want to be the reason for any negativity.

One day, Rachel was tasked with leading a new project for the company. It was a huge opportunity for her to showcase her skills and potential, but it also came with a lot of pressure. Rachel could have easily let stress and doubt cloud her judgment, but she chose to stay positive and focused on the task at hand.

She worked tirelessly to come up with creative ideas and strategies, and she always kept an open mind to feedback and suggestions from her team. She was also proactive in seeking out resources and support when needed.

As the project progressed, Rachel's positive attitude began to rub off on her team members. They were all more motivated and inspired to do their best work, and the results reflected that. The project was a huge success, and Rachel received high praise from her superiors.

It wasn't long before Rachel was promoted to a leadership role within the marketing team. She was thrilled to have the opportunity to take on more responsibilities and make an even bigger impact at the company.

Looking back, Rachel realized that her positive attitude played a crucial role in her success. It had helped her to overcome challenges, build strong relationships with her team, and ultimately earn the promotion she had been striving for.

Rachel's story serves as a reminder that a positive attitude can truly make all the difference in our careers and personal lives. It's not always easy to maintain a positive outlook, but the benefits are well worth the effort.

3. RELATIONSHIP BUILDING

Building relationships at work can greatly aid job promotion and career advancement. In today's competitive job market, it is not just about what you know, but who you know and how well you get along with others. Building strong relationships with your colleagues, supervisors, and even clients can open doors to new opportunities and increase your chances of getting promoted.

One way that relationship building can aid in promotion is by increasing your visibility within the company. By forming strong connections with your coworkers, you are more likely to be noticed by higher-ups and become a valuable member of the team. When it comes time for promotions, those who have developed positive relationships with their colleagues are often given more consideration than those who have not.

Additionally, building relationships can also increase your credibility within the company. When you have a good rapport with your coworkers, it can make you more trustworthy and reliable. This can lead to being given more responsibility and the opportunity to take on higher-level tasks, which can ultimately lead to promotion.

Another way that relationship building can aid in promotion is by helping you network within the company. By getting to know your colleagues and building strong relationships with them, you have the opportunity to learn about potential job openings and have the support of your colleagues when it comes time to apply. This can give you a competitive advantage over other candidates who may not have the same level of connections within the company.

In addition to networking within the company, building relationships with clients can also be beneficial for promotion. By developing strong relationships with clients, you can showcase your skills and work ethic, which can lead to being given more responsibility and the opportunity for promotion.

However, it is important to note that building relationships at work does not mean compromising your values or integrity. It is important to be authentic and genuine in your interactions with others, as insincerity can ultimately harm your reputation and career advancement.

In conclusion, building relationships at work can greatly aid in promotion and career advancement. By increasing your visibility within the company, increasing your credibility, networking within the company, and developing strong relationships with clients, you can open doors to new opportunities and increase your chances of getting promoted. It is important to remember to be authentic and genuine in your interactions with others, as insincerity can ultimately harm your reputation and career advancement.

SCENARIO...
It was a typical Monday morning at the office when Jerry walked into the conference room for his weekly meeting with his boss, Lisa. As he sat

down, he couldn't help but feel a sense of nervousness wash over him. Jerry had been working for the company for five years now, and he had always dreamed of being promoted to a managerial position. However, despite his hard work and dedication, he had yet to be recognized for his potential.

As the meeting began, Lisa went over the usual updates and discussed upcoming projects. But as the conversation turned to Jerry's performance, he couldn't help but hold his breath. Would this be the moment he had been waiting for?

"Jerry, I wanted to talk to you about your career progression here at the company," Lisa said, looking at him with a serious expression. "I know you've been with us for a while now and you've consistently put in a lot of hard work. But I have to be honest,

I've been hesitant to promote you because I've noticed that you tend to keep to yourself and don't really engage with your colleagues."

Jerry's heart sank. He had always been a bit of an introvert and struggled with building relationships with his coworkers. He had always thought that as long as he was doing his job well, that would be enough. But now he realized that he had been wrong.

Determined to turn things around, Jerry decided to focus on building relationships with his colleagues. He started by making an effort to be more social at the office, joining in on team lunches and happy hours. He also made an effort to get to know his coworkers on a personal level, asking about their hobbies and interests outside of work.

As Jerry started to build stronger relationships with his coworkers, he noticed a change in his own behavior. He found himself feeling more confident and motivated, and his work started to reflect that. He began to take on more responsibilities and was always willing to help out wherever he could.

As his relationships with his colleagues improved, Jerry's boss noticed a change in him as well. Lisa commented on how much more engaged he seemed in his work and how he was always willing to go above and beyond. It wasn't long before Jerry was finally given the promotion he had been working towards.

As he sat in his new office, Jerry couldn't help but feel grateful for the relationships he had built with his coworkers. He realized that building relationships at work wasn't just about making friends, it was about creating a positive and supportive work environment. And it was this focus on relationship building that helped him to finally reach his goal of becoming a manager.

4. WORK ETHICS

A good work ethic is an essential component of success in any career. It is the foundation upon which all other skills and abilities are built, and is a key factor in determining whether or not an individual will be successful in their job. In order to gain promotion at work, it is necessary to demonstrate a strong work ethic and a commitment to excellence in everything you do.

So, what exactly is a good work ethic and how can it be developed and demonstrated in the workplace? A good work ethic is characterized by several key traits, including:

Responsibility: A good work ethic means being reliable and dependable, and taking ownership of your work. This means being punctual, meeting deadlines, and being accountable for your actions. It also means being proactive and proactive in identifying and solving problems, and not waiting for someone else to fix things for you.

Hard work: A good work ethic means being willing to put in the effort and time necessary to get the job done. This means being diligent, persistent, and consistently striving to improve your skills and knowledge. It also means being willing to take on additional responsibilities and tasks when needed, and not shying away from challenges.

Positive attitude: A good work ethic also means having a positive attitude and being a team player. This means being respectful and cooperative with colleagues, and being willing to lend a helping hand when needed. It also means being able to handle criticism and feedback constructively, and being open to learning and growing from it.

Professionalism: A good work ethic means being professional in all aspects of your job, from your appearance and demeanor to your communication and interactions with others. This means dressing appropriately, being polite and courteous, and maintaining a professional demeanor at all times.

Adaptability: A good work ethic means being able to adapt to new situations and challenges, and being willing to learn and grow as needed. This means being open to change, and being able to adjust your work style and approach as needed.

To demonstrate a good work ethic and increase your chances of gaining promotion at work, it is important to consistently exhibit these traits on a daily basis. This means going above and beyond in your job duties, and always striving for excellence. Additionally, it is important to communicate your good work ethic to your supervisor and other key decision makers within the organization. This can be done through a variety of methods, such as:

Performance reviews: Performance reviews are an excellent opportunity to showcase your good work ethic and accomplishments. Be sure to highlight any specific projects or tasks you have taken on, and any successes or improvements you have made in your job.

Asking for feedback: Asking for feedback is a great way to show your commitment to improvement and learning. By actively seeking out feedback from your supervisor and other colleagues, you can demonstrate your willingness to learn and grow in your role.

Networking: Networking is an important aspect of any career, and can be a great way to showcase your good work ethic and build relationships with key decision makers within the organization. Be sure to attend company events and industry conferences, and take advantage of any networking opportunities that arise.

Professional development: Investing in your own professional development is a great way to demonstrate your commitment to your career and your good work ethic. Consider taking courses or obtaining certifications that will help you grow and improve in your job.

By consistently demonstrating a good work ethic and a commitment to excellence in your work, you will be well on your way to gaining promotion in your workplace.

SCENARIO...
It was a around 8am when John walked into the office, ready to start another week of work. As he settled into his desk and began sorting through his emails, he couldn't help but feel a sense of dread wash over him. Despite his hard work and dedication, John had been passed

over for promotion multiple times in the past, and he was starting to lose hope that he would ever be recognized for his efforts.

But John was determined not to let his frustrations get the best of him. He knew that he had the skills and experience to excel in his role, and he was determined to show his boss and colleagues just how valuable he was to the team. So he set to work, putting in extra hours and going above and beyond on every project that came his way.

At first, John's efforts seemed to go unnoticed. He was still getting the same workload as before, and he wasn't seeing any tangible results from his hard work. But he didn't let this discourage him. He continued to stay focused and motivated, always striving to do his best and be the best teammate he could be.

Over time, John's dedication began to pay off. His colleagues started to take notice of his hard work and dedication, and he was frequently called upon to take on more responsibilities and lead important projects. His boss also took notice, and he started to see John as a valuable asset to the team.

Eventually, John's hard work and dedication were recognized with a well-deserved promotion. He was thrilled and grateful to have finally been recognized for his efforts, and he knew that it was his strong work ethic that had helped him get to where he was.

From then on, John continued to excel in his new role, always striving to be the best employee he could be. He remained dedicated and focused, always willing to put in the extra effort to get the job done. And his colleagues and boss continued to take notice, leading to even more promotions and opportunities for growth within the company.

Looking back, John knew that he had come a long way from those early days of feeling overlooked and unappreciated. It was his determination and work ethic that helped him overcome those obstacles and reach new heights in his career. And he was proud to be able to inspire others to do the same, knowing that with hard work and dedication, anything was possible.

5. PERSUASION SKILL

Persuasion skills are essential for success in the workplace, particularly when it comes to seeking promotion. These skills allow individuals to effectively communicate their ideas, influence decision making, and build strong relationships with their colleagues and superiors.

Here are just a few ways in which persuasion skills can aid promotion at work:

Clearly communicating your goals and aspirations: When seeking promotion, it's important to clearly communicate your goals and aspirations to your superiors. This means outlining your strengths, skills, and experiences that make you a strong candidate for the position. Persuasion skills can help you present this information in a clear and compelling manner, making it more likely that your superiors will consider you for the promotion.

Building strong relationships with your colleagues: Persuasion skills are also essential for building strong relationships with your colleagues. This is important because your colleagues can be a valuable source of support when you're seeking promotion. By persuading them to support your goals and aspirations, you can increase your chances of getting the promotion you desire.

Influencing decision making: Persuasion skills are also valuable for influencing decision making. Whether you're trying to persuade your superiors to consider you for a promotion or you're trying to persuade your colleagues to support your ideas, effective persuasion skills can help you make a strong case for your viewpoint.

Demonstrating your value to the company: When seeking promotion, it's important to demonstrate your value to the company. This means highlighting the skills and experiences that make you an asset to the organization. Persuasion skills can help you effectively communicate this value to your superiors, making it more likely that they will consider you for a promotion.

Negotiating salary and benefits: Persuasion skills are also essential for negotiating salary and benefits. When you're seeking promotion, it's important to negotiate a salary and benefits package that reflects your value to the organization. By persuading your superiors to offer you a fair and competitive package, you can increase your chances of getting the promotion you desire.

Overall, persuasion skills are an essential component of success in the workplace, particularly when it comes to seeking promotion. By effectively communicating your goals and aspirations, building strong relationships with your colleagues, influencing decision making, demonstrating your value to the company, and negotiating salary and benefits, you can increase your chances of getting the promotion you desire.

SCENARIO...
As an employee at a large corporation, Mary had always been ambitious and eager to advance in her career. She had worked hard for years, taking on extra projects and going above and beyond in her duties.
Frustrated and determined to succeed, Mary decided to take a closer look at her colleagues who had been promoted. She noticed that they all seemed to possess one common trait: strong persuasion skills.

Determined to improve in this area, Mary began studying the art of persuasion and practiced every chance she got. She learned about the power of body language, the importance of building rapport, and the art of framing arguments in a way that was compelling and convincing.

As she grew more confident in her persuasion skills, Mary began to apply them in her everyday work. She began to speak up more in meetings, presenting her ideas and opinions in a clear and concise manner. She also made a point to listen actively to her colleagues and engage in respectful, open-minded discussions.

As a result, Mary began to gain a reputation as a confident and persuasive team member. Her superiors took notice and began to see her as a valuable asset to the company.

Finally, the opportunity for promotion arose, and Mary was determined to make the most of it. She put together a well-crafted, persuasive presentation outlining her qualifications and ideas for the new role. She practiced her delivery and made sure to use all of the persuasion techniques she had learned.

When it came time for the presentation, Mary was a natural. She spoke confidently and clearly, making a strong case for why she was the best candidate for the promotion. She listened attentively to the feedback and questions of her superiors, and was able to address their concerns with well thought-out responses.

In the end, Mary's persistence and dedication to improving her persuasion skills paid off. She was offered the promotion and accepted it with gratitude and excitement.

From that point on, Mary continued to use her persuasion skills to excel in her new role and climb the corporate ladder. She became known as a strong leader and a valuable asset to the company, all thanks to her ability to persuade and convince others.

Mary's story is a testament to the power of persuasion in the workplace. By developing these skills and applying them with determination and hard work, anyone can achieve their career goals and reach new heights of success.

6. NEGOTIATION SKILL

Negotiation skills are crucial in achieving career advancement and success in the workplace. By being able to effectively negotiate, employees can secure promotions, raise, better working conditions, and other benefits that can help them progress in their careers.

Here are some ways in which good negotiation skills can aid promotion at work:

Improved communication: Good negotiation skills involve being able to effectively communicate one's needs, wants, and expectations. By being able to clearly articulate their goals and concerns, employees can build trust and credibility with their superiors and colleagues, which can increase the chances of being considered for a promotion.

Conflict resolution: The ability to resolve conflicts and reach mutually beneficial solutions is an essential part of negotiation. By showing that they can handle difficult situations and find solutions that work for everyone, employees can demonstrate their leadership skills and potential for advancement.

Building relationships: Negotiation skills involve building and maintaining relationships with others. By being able to work effectively with their colleagues and superiors, employees can create a positive work environment and improve their chances of being promoted.

Assertiveness: Good negotiation skills involve being able to assert oneself in a respectful and professional manner. By being able to stand up for oneself and advocate for their own interests, employees can demonstrate their value and worth to their employer and increase their chances of being promoted.

Adaptability: Good negotiation skills involve being able to adapt to different situations and find solutions that work for all parties involved. By showing that they can be flexible and adapt to changing circumstances, employees can demonstrate their ability to handle new challenges and responsibilities, which can increase the chances of being promoted.

In conclusion, good negotiation skills are essential for career advancement and success in the workplace. By being able to effectively communicate, resolve conflicts, build relationships, assert oneself, and adapt to different situations, employees can increase their chances of being promoted and succeed in their careers.

SCENARIO…
It was a typical Monday morning at the office when John received the news that he had been waiting for. His

GOING UP?

boss, Mr. Johnson, called him into his office and informed him that he was being considered for a promotion. John was overjoyed at the opportunity, but he knew that he would have to prove himself worthy of the new position.

Over the next few weeks, John worked tirelessly to prove himself. He put in extra hours and went above and beyond in all of his assignments. He made sure to always be on top of his work and to be a valuable member of the team.

But as the days went by, John began to worry. He had heard that there were several other candidates being considered for the promotion, and he knew that he would have to do something extra to stand out.

One day, while discussing the promotion with a colleague, John had an idea. He realized that he could use his good negotiation skills to his advantage. He decided to sit down with Mr. Johnson and discuss his qualifications for the promotion in detail.

John began by outlining all of his accomplishments and successes at the company. He highlighted his strong work ethic and his dedication to the company's goals. He also pointed out his willingness to go above and beyond and his ability to work well with others.

But John didn't stop there. He also discussed his long-term goals and how the promotion would help him achieve them. He made it clear that he was committed to the company and that he wanted to continue growing with the company.

Mr. Johnson was impressed by John's presentation and his willingness to negotiate. He knew that John was the right candidate for the promotion and he offered him the position on the spot.

John was overjoyed at the news and he knew that his good negotiation skills had played a big part in his success. He was grateful for the opportunity and he knew that he would work even harder to live up to the expectations of his new position.

As John continued to excel in his new role, he became a valuable asset to the company. He was able to use his negotiation skills to secure important deals and contracts, and he quickly became one of the company's most valuable employees.

Over the years, John continued to climb the corporate ladder and he eventually became the CEO of the company. He knew that he wouldn't have gotten there without his good negotiation skills, and he was grateful for the opportunity that they had given him.

As John looked back on his journey, he knew that his good negotiation skills had been the key to his success. They had helped him to gain the promotion that he had been working towards and they had helped him to achieve his long-term goals. He was grateful for the skills that he had acquired and he knew that they would continue to serve him well in the future.

7. TEAMWORK

Teamwork is the ability to work together towards a common goal. It is an essential element in any organization, as it enables individuals to collaborate effectively and achieve results that they may not be able to accomplish on their own. In the workplace, teamwork can aid promotion in several ways.

First and foremost, teamwork fosters a sense of unity and cooperation among team members. When employees work together and support each other, they are more likely to develop a positive and productive work environment. This is especially important in situations where team members are required to work under tight deadlines or handle high levels of stress. By working together and supporting each other, team members can overcome challenges and achieve success.

In addition to promoting a positive work environment, teamwork also helps employees to develop valuable skills and knowledge. When team members work together, they are exposed to different perspectives and ideas, which can help them to learn and grow. For example, if one team member is skilled in a particular area, they may be able to share their expertise with others, enabling them to learn and improve their skills. This is especially valuable for employees who are looking to advance in their careers and take on new responsibilities.

Teamwork can also aid promotion by increasing efficiency and productivity. When team members work together, they can divide tasks and responsibilities, allowing them to complete projects more quickly and efficiently. This is especially useful in situations where there are multiple projects or tasks that need to be completed simultaneously. By working together and dividing tasks, team members can avoid duplication of effort and ensure that all tasks are completed in a timely manner.

In addition to increasing efficiency and productivity, teamwork can also help to reduce conflict and improve communication in the workplace. When team members work together and communicate effectively, they are more likely to understand each other's needs and goals, which can help to resolve conflicts before they escalate. This is especially important in situations where team members may have different priorities or objectives. By working together and communicating effectively, team members can ensure that everyone is on the same page and working towards a common goal.

Finally, teamwork can aid promotion by increasing employee satisfaction and motivation. When team members feel like they are a part of a team and are valued for their contributions, they are more likely to feel motivated and engaged in their work. This is especially important for employees who are looking to advance in their careers, as a positive work environment and strong team dynamic can be a key factor in determining whether an employee feels motivated to take on new challenges and responsibilities.

In conclusion, teamwork is a crucial element in any organization, as it enables individuals to collaborate effectively and achieve results that they may not be able to accomplish on their own. In the workplace, teamwork can aid promotion in several ways, including fostering a positive work environment, developing valuable skills and knowledge, increasing efficiency and productivity, reducing conflict and improving communication, and increasing employee satisfaction and motivation.

SCENARIO...

It was a typical Monday morning at the office and Jane was feeling anxious as she sat at her desk. She had been working at the company for three years and had always dreamed of being promoted to a higher position. However, despite her hard work and dedication, she had yet to receive any recognition or advancement.

As she rummaged through her work, her boss, Mr. Smith, approached her. "Jane, can I speak with you for a moment?" he asked.

Jane's heart skipped a beat as she stood up and followed Mr. Smith into his office. "What's this about?" she asked nervously.

"Well," Mr. Smith began, "I've noticed your hard work and dedication to this company over the years and I think it's time for you to be recognized for your efforts. I'm offering you a promotion to team leader."

Jane was overjoyed and couldn't believe her ears. "Thank you so much, Mr. Smith," she exclaimed. "I won't let you down."

As she returned to her desk, Jane couldn't help but think about how teamwork had played a major role in her promotion. She had always been a team player, working closely with her coworkers and helping them whenever they needed it. This teamwork had not only helped to complete tasks efficiently, but it had also gained her the respect and admiration of her colleagues.

In her new position as team leader, Jane continued to focus on teamwork and communication within the team. She held regular meetings to discuss projects and assign tasks, ensuring that everyone was on the same page and working towards the same goals.

In addition to her leadership skills, Jane also made a point to recognize the hard work and efforts of her team members. She would often praise them for their contributions and would offer words of encouragement when they faced challenges. This positive reinforcement helped to boost the morale of the team and resulted in an increase in productivity.

As the months went by, Jane's team began to thrive under her leadership. They were consistently meeting deadlines and exceeding expectations, and their work was being recognized by upper management.

It was no surprise when Jane was once again offered a promotion, this time to a managerial position. She accepted the offer with gratitude and continued to lead her team with a focus on teamwork and communication.

Looking back, Jane couldn't believe how far she had come in just a few short years. She knew that it was the teamwork and support of her colleagues that had helped her to gain these promotions and succeed in her career. She was grateful for the opportunity and excited for what the future held.

8. EMOTIONAL INTELLIGENCE

Emotional intelligence is the ability to recognize and understand one's own emotions and the emotions of others, as well as to use this awareness to manage behavior and relationships effectively. This skill can be particularly important in the workplace, as it can not only improve individual performance but also facilitate better teamwork and leadership.

One way in which emotional intelligence can aid promotion at work is by improving communication and interpersonal skills. When employees are able to recognize and manage their emotions, they are more likely to be able to listen actively and communicate effectively with their colleagues. This can lead to more productive and harmonious working relationships, which can be beneficial for the entire team.

Another way in which emotional intelligence can aid promotion at work is by enabling employees to adapt to change and handle stress more effectively. The ability to recognize and manage one's emotions can help individuals to stay calm and focused in the face of challenges or setbacks, rather than becoming overwhelmed or reactive. This can be especially important in fast-paced or high-stress environments, where the ability to remain composed and level-headed can be a valuable asset.

Emotional intelligence can also enhance leadership skills, as it allows individuals to understand and respond appropriately to the emotions of their team members. For example, a leader with high emotional intelligence might be able to recognize when a team member is feeling overwhelmed or frustrated, and provide support and guidance to help them overcome these challenges. This can help to build trust and respect within the team, which can be essential for building a positive and productive work culture.

Finally, emotional intelligence can aid promotion at work by improving decision-making skills. When individuals are able to recognize and understand their own emotions, they are better able to evaluate the potential consequences of their actions and make more thoughtful and considered decisions. This can be especially valuable in leadership roles, where the ability to make sound judgments can be critical to the success of the team or organization.

Overall, emotional intelligence can be a powerful tool for enhancing performance and facilitating promotion at work. By recognizing and managing emotions effectively, individuals can improve their communication and interpersonal skills, adapt to change and handle stress more effectively, enhance their leadership abilities, and make more thoughtful and considerate decisions. These skills can not only benefit individual employees, but also contribute to a more positive and productive work environment for the entire team or organization.

SCENARIO...

Sarah had always been a hard worker, but she struggled to get ahead in her career. She was passed up for promotions time and time again, despite putting in long hours and consistently meeting her goals. Frustrated and discouraged, Sarah began to feel like she would never reach the level of success she desired.

One day, Sarah's manager suggested she attend a training seminar on emotional intelligence. Initially, Sarah was hesitant. She had always thought of herself as a logical and rational person, and the idea of focusing on her emotions seemed like a waste of time. But eventually, she decided to give it a try.

The seminar was led by a dynamic speaker who introduced Sarah to the concept of emotional intelligence. He explained that emotional intelligence was the ability to recognize and manage one's own emotions and the emotions of others. He went on to say that individuals with high emotional intelligence tend to be more successful in their careers because they are better able to navigate complex social situations and communicate effectively with their coworkers and supervisors.

Sarah was intrigued by this new concept and decided to start applying the principles of emotional intelligence to her work. She began by learning to manage her own emotions, making a conscious effort to regulate her mood and stay focused on her tasks. She also worked on improving her ability to read and respond to the emotions of others, paying attention to nonverbal cues and actively listening to her coworkers and supervisors.

As Sarah began to implement these strategies, she noticed a significant shift in her work environment. Her relationships with her coworkers improved, as she was able to better understand and support their needs. She also found that she was able to more effectively communicate with her supervisors, and her productivity increased as a result.

As the months went by, Sarah's manager took notice of the changes in her behavior and performance. She was eventually offered a promotion to a leadership role, which she eagerly accepted. Sarah was thrilled to finally have the opportunity to advance in her career, and she knew that her newfound emotional intelligence had played a crucial role in her success.

Over the next few years, Sarah continued to develop her emotional intelligence, and her career continued to thrive. She was respected and admired by her coworkers, and she was able to effectively lead and motivate her team. She had finally achieved the success she had always dreamed of, and she knew that it was all thanks to the skills she had learned in that seminar on emotional intelligence.

Sarah's story is a testament to the power of emotional intelligence in the workplace. By learning to recognize and manage her own emotions and the emotions of others, she was able to improve her communication and relationships, leading to a successful and fulfilling career. Sarah's experience serves as a reminder of the importance of emotional intelligence in achieving success in any field. Sarah had always been a hard worker, but she struggled to get ahead in her career. She was passed up for promotions time and time again, despite putting in long hours and consistently meeting her goals. Frustrated and discouraged, Sarah began to feel like she would never reach the level of success she desired.

One day, Sarah's manager suggested she attend a training seminar on emotional intelligence. Initially, Sarah was hesitant. She had always thought of herself as a logical and rational person, and the idea of focusing on her emotions seemed like a waste of time. But eventually, she decided to give it a try.

The seminar was led by a dynamic speaker who introduced Sarah to the concept of emotional intelligence. He explained that emotional intelligence was the ability to recognize and manage one's own emotions and the emotions of others. He went on to say that individuals with high emotional intelligence tend to be more successful in their careers because they are better able to navigate complex social situations and communicate effectively with their coworkers and supervisors.

Sarah was intrigued by this new concept and decided to start applying the principles of emotional intelligence to her work. She began by learning to manage her own emotions, making a conscious effort to regulate her mood and stay focused on her tasks. She also worked on improving her ability to read and respond to the emotions of others, paying attention to nonverbal cues and actively listening to her coworkers and supervisors.

As Sarah began to implement these strategies, she noticed a significant shift in her work environment. Her relationships with her coworkers improved, as she was able to better understand and support their needs. She also found that she was able to more effectively communicate with her supervisors, and her productivity increased as a result.

As the months went by, Sarah's manager took notice of the changes in her behavior and performance. She was eventually offered a promotion to a leadership role, which she eagerly accepted. Sarah was thrilled to finally have the opportunity to advance in her career, and she knew that her newfound emotional intelligence had played a crucial role in her success.

Over the next few years, Sarah continued to develop her emotional intelligence, and her career continued to thrive. She was respected and admired by her coworkers, and she was able to effectively lead and motivate her team. She had finally achieved the success she had always dreamed of, and she knew that it was all thanks to the skills she had learned in that seminar on emotional intelligence.

Sarah's story is a testament to the power of emotional intelligence in the workplace. By learning to recognize and manage her own emotions and the emotions of others, she was able to improve her communication and relationships, leading to a successful and fulfilling career. Sarah's experience serves as a reminder of the importance of emotional intelligence in achieving success in any field.

9. EMPATHY

Empathy is the ability to understand and share the feelings of another person. It is a crucial skill that can greatly aid in promotion at work, as it allows individuals to better connect with their colleagues and clients, build stronger relationships, and effectively communicate and collaborate with others.

One way that empathy can aid in promotion at work is through improved communication and collaboration. When individuals are able to understand and share the emotions of their colleagues and clients, they are better able to see things from their perspective and effectively communicate with them. This can lead to more productive and efficient meetings, as well as better outcomes for projects and tasks. Additionally, the ability to empathize allows individuals to better collaborate with others, as they are able to understand and work with the emotions and needs of their team members.

Another way that empathy can aid in promotion at work is through the development of stronger relationships. When individuals are able to show empathy towards their colleagues and clients, they are able to build stronger and more positive relationships. This can lead to a more cohesive and collaborative work environment, as well as increased trust and respect among team members. Additionally, strong relationships can lead to increased loyalty and support among colleagues, which can be beneficial when seeking promotions or other opportunities within the company.

Empathy can also aid in promotion at work by helping individuals to better handle difficult situations and conflicts. When individuals are able to understand and share the emotions of others, they are better able to find solutions to problems and resolve conflicts in a more effective and compassionate manner. This ability to handle difficult situations in a calm and empathetic manner can be highly valued by employers and can lead to increased opportunities for promotion.

In addition to the benefits for individuals, empathy can also have positive impacts on a company as a whole. A work environment that values and promotes empathy can lead to increased job satisfaction and productivity, as well as better outcomes for projects and tasks. This can ultimately lead to the success and growth of the company, which can provide opportunities for promotions and advancement for all employees.

Overall, empathy is a valuable skill that can greatly aid in promotion at work. It allows individuals to better connect with their colleagues and clients, build stronger relationships, and effectively communicate and collaborate with others. Additionally, it can help individuals to handle difficult situations and conflicts in a more effective and compassionate manner, and can lead to a more cohesive and successful work environment for all.

SCENARIO...

It was a typical day at the office and Lucy was feeling overwhelmed as she sat at her desk, staring at the pile of work in front of her. She had been working at the company for the past three years and had always been a reliable and hardworking employee, but she felt like she was constantly being passed over for promotions.

As she sat there feeling sorry for herself, her boss, Mrs. Thompson, walked by and asked if she had a moment to talk. Lucy's heart sank, thinking that she was in trouble, but Mrs. Thompson sat down and told her that she had noticed her dedication and hard work and wanted to offer her a promotion to team leader.

Lucy was shocked and couldn't believe what she was hearing. She asked Mrs. Thompson what had led to this decision and Mrs. Thompson told her that it was her empathy and ability to connect with her coworkers that had really stood out.

Lucy was a natural empath and had always been able to sense the emotions of those around her, but she had never really thought about how that could benefit her at work. She had always just tried to be a good listener and support her coworkers when they were going through a tough time, but she had never realized the impact it was having on her career.

Mrs. Thompson explained that Lucy's empathy had helped her to build strong relationships with her coworkers and created a positive and collaborative work environment. It had also helped her to be a more effective leader, as she was able to understand and address the needs and concerns of her team.

Lucy was overwhelmed with gratitude and couldn't believe that her natural ability to connect with others had helped her to gain this promotion. She knew that she had always been a hard worker, but she had never realized the value of empathy in the workplace.

From that day on, Lucy made a conscious effort to use her empathy to connect with her coworkers and understand their needs. She became a more effective leader and was able to inspire her team to work together and achieve great things.

As the years went on, Lucy's career continued to thrive and she was consistently recognized for her leadership and ability to connect with others. She was grateful for the lesson that empathy can be a powerful tool in the workplace and made sure to always use it to her advantage.

10. TIME MANAGEMENT

Time management is an essential skill that can have a significant impact on your career success, particularly when it comes to promotion at work. By effectively managing your time, you can increase your productivity, meet deadlines, and achieve your career goals. In this essay, we will explore how time management can aid promotion at work and discuss several strategies for effectively managing your time.

First, it's important to understand why time management is so important in the workplace. In today's fast-paced business environment, there is often a lot of pressure to get things done quickly and efficiently. If you are able to manage your time effectively, you will be able to meet deadlines and complete tasks efficiently, which can help you stand out in the workplace. Additionally, good time management skills can help you avoid feeling overwhelmed and stressed, which can have a negative impact on your overall performance.

One key strategy for effective time management is setting clear goals and priorities. By knowing what you need to accomplish and prioritizing your tasks, you can ensure that you are focusing on the most important work and using your time effectively. It can be helpful to create a to-do list or schedule to help you keep track of your tasks and stay organized.

Another important aspect of time management is avoiding distractions. This can be challenging in today's digital age, with constant notifications and the temptation to check social media or emails. It's important to minimize distractions and focus on your work to make the most of your time. This can involve setting aside dedicated blocks of time for focused work, using tools like website blockers to limit your access to distracting websites, and finding a quiet place to work if possible.

Effective time management also involves being proactive and taking control of your schedule. This can involve setting boundaries and saying no to commitments that will take up too much of your time or energy. It can also involve delegating tasks to others or seeking out ways to streamline your workflow to be more efficient.

In addition to the strategies mentioned above, there are several other time management techniques that can be helpful in the workplace. These include:

Batching similar tasks together: By grouping similar tasks together, you can be more efficient and avoid switching between different types of work.

Time blocking: This involves scheduling specific blocks of time for specific tasks or activities. This can help you stay focused and avoid feeling overwhelmed.

The Pomodoro Technique: This involves working for a set period of time (such as 25 minutes) and then taking a short break (such as 5 minutes). This can help you stay focused and avoid burnout.

Using technology to your advantage: There are many tools and apps available that can help you manage your time more effectively, such as project management software, calendar apps, and time-tracking tools.

In conclusion, time management is an essential skill that can greatly aid promotion at work. By setting clear goals, avoiding distractions, taking control of your schedule, and using various time management techniques, you can increase your productivity, meet deadlines, and achieve your career goals. By mastering these skills, you can set yourself up for success and position yourself for promotions in the future.

SCENARIO...
It was the first day of the month for John, a middle-aged employee at a local software company. He sat at his desk, sipping his coffee and scrolling through his emails, trying to mentally prepare for the long day ahead.

As he sorted through his inbox, he noticed a message from his boss, requesting a meeting at 10 am to discuss John's recent performance. John's heart sank. He had been feeling overwhelmed at work lately, constantly struggling to meet deadlines and keep up with his workload. He knew that this meeting was likely a warning of some sort, and he dreaded the thought of being reprimanded or even fired.

Determined to turn things around, John made a decision. He would make time management his top priority. He knew that if he could get a handle on his schedule and become more organized, he could improve his performance and hopefully save his job.

John began by setting specific goals for each day and breaking them down into smaller tasks. He also created a schedule, outlining what he needed to accomplish and when. This helped him to stay focused and avoid wasting time on unimportant tasks.

In addition to this, John also learned the importance of prioritizing his work. He realized that not all tasks were equal in importance, and he needed to focus on the most important ones first. He learned to delegate tasks to his coworkers when appropriate and say no to any requests that would take away from his ability to complete his own work.

As the weeks went by, John noticed a significant improvement in his performance. He was meeting deadlines and exceeding expectations. His boss noticed this too and began to take notice of John's efforts.

One day, John received an email from his boss requesting a meeting. This time, however, John wasn't worried. He knew he had been working hard and improving his time management skills, and he was confident that he was ready for whatever his boss had to say.

At the meeting, John's boss congratulated him on his improved performance and announced that he was being promoted to team leader. John was overjoyed at the news and couldn't believe that all his hard work had paid off.

As he left the meeting, John couldn't help but feel grateful for the struggles he had faced earlier in the year. They had pushed him to make a change and improve his time management skills, and that change had ultimately led to his promotion.

From then on, John continued to use his time management skills to excel in his new position and lead his team to success. He realized that by taking control of his schedule and prioritizing his work, he was able to not only save his job but also advance his career.

John learned that time management was not only crucial for success at work but in life as well. He made it a habit to regularly review and adjust his schedule to ensure that he was using his time wisely and efficiently. And he knew that with hard work and dedication, he could continue to achieve great things in his career and beyond.

11. PROBLEM-SOLVING SKILLS

Problem solving skills are essential for success in the workplace, as they enable individuals to identify and resolve issues that arise in a timely and effective manner. These skills are especially valuable in the promotion process, as they demonstrate an employee's ability to take initiative and leadership, as well as their capacity to think critically and make informed decisions.

One of the key ways in which problem-solving skills can aid

promotion in the workplace is by enabling employees to identify and address problems before they become major issues. For example, if an employee is able to identify a potential problem with a project, they can work to resolve it before it becomes a major hindrance to the team's progress. This not only demonstrates their problem-solving ability, but also their ability to think proactively and take initiative. This type of proactive problem-solving can be highly valued by managers and can help to set an employee apart from their peers when it comes to promotion opportunities.

In addition to identifying and addressing problems before they become major issues, problem-solving skills can also help employees to effectively resolve issues that do arise. This may involve working with others to find creative solutions to complex problems, or using analytical and critical thinking skills to come up with innovative solutions. When employees are able to effectively resolve problems, they demonstrate their value to the organization and their ability to contribute to the success of the team. This can be a key factor in the promotion process, as it shows that an employee has the skills and abilities necessary to take on additional responsibilities and contribute to the organization's success at a higher level.

Problem-solving skills can also help employees to communicate effectively and work collaboratively with others. In many cases, solving problems in the workplace requires input and collaboration from multiple individuals, and having strong communication skills is essential for success. When employees are able to clearly and effectively communicate their ideas and work effectively with others to solve problems, they demonstrate their ability to contribute to the team and work well with others. This is often highly valued by managers and can be a key factor in the promotion process.

In addition to these more practical benefits, problem-solving skills can also have a positive impact on an employee's overall job performance and satisfaction. When employees are able to effectively identify and resolve problems, they are likely to feel more confident and competent in their work, which can lead to higher levels of job satisfaction and engagement. This, can lead to better performance and increased productivity, which can be valuable factors in the promotion process.

Overall, problem-solving skills are essential for success in the workplace and can be a major factor in the promotion process. By enabling employees to identify and resolve problems, communicate effectively with others, and contribute to the team's success, problem-solving skills can help employees to stand out and advance in their careers. As such, it is important for employees to continue to develop and hone their problem-solving skills throughout their careers in order to maximize their potential for success and advancement.

SCENARIO...
As an employee, problem solving skills are an essential part of being successful in the workplace. The ability to identify problems, come up with creative solutions, and implement those solutions effectively can be the difference between being stuck in a dead-end job and climbing the corporate ladder.

One employee who exemplified this was Rachel, a mid-level manager at a tech company. Rachel had always been a hard worker, but she struggled to stand out in a competitive industry. She was determined to earn a promotion, but she knew she needed to demonstrate her problem solving skills in order to do so.

Rachel began by identifying areas in the company where problems were occurring. She noticed that there was a high rate of employee turnover in the customer service department, and she suspected that it might be due to poor training and support. She decided to take on this issue as a project, determined to find a solution.

First, Rachel gathered data on the issue, collecting information on the types of complaints that were most common and the specific issues that seemed to be causing employees to leave. She also surveyed current and former employees to get their insights on the problem.

Using this data, Rachel was able to identify the root cause of the high turnover rate: inadequate training and support. She knew that she needed to come up with a solution that would address these issues and improve the overall customer experience.

Rachel spent several weeks researching and brainstorming potential solutions, and she eventually came up with a comprehensive plan to overhaul the customer service training and support program. She presented her plan to her superiors, highlighting the benefits it would bring to both the company and its employees.

Her superiors were impressed with the level of thought and effort Rachel had put into her proposal, and they decided to implement her plan. The results were immediate and dramatic. Customer satisfaction levels soared, and employee turnover in the customer service department plummeted.

Rachel's success in solving this problem caught the attention of her superiors, and she was soon offered a promotion to a higher-level management position. She was thrilled to have the opportunity to take on more responsibility and continue making a positive impact on the company.

Throughout her career, Rachel continued to use her problem solving skills to tackle a variety of issues and challenges. She became known as an invaluable asset to her company, and she continued to earn promotions and recognition for her contributions.

In the end, Rachel's ability to identify problems, come up with creative solutions, and implement those solutions effectively was the key to her success. It was her problem solving skills that helped her stand out in the competitive tech industry and earn the promotions she deserved.

12. ADAPTABILITY

Adaptability is a crucial skill that can significantly aid in career progression and promotion in the workplace. It is the ability to adapt to new situations, environments, or challenges, and to quickly learn and apply new skills and knowledge. It is a key competency that enables employees to thrive in an increasingly dynamic and fast-paced business world.

In today's rapidly changing business environment, adaptability is more important than ever. With constant technological advancements, shifting market conditions, and changing customer needs, organizations must be able to adapt and innovate in order to remain competitive. Employees who are adaptable are able to adapt to these changes and take on new challenges, which is essential for their own professional growth and development, as well as the success of their organization.

One of the primary benefits of adaptability is the ability to learn and grow. Employees who are adaptable are able to continuously learn and develop new skills, which can make them more valuable to their organization. This not only enhances their own career prospects, but also helps their organization stay ahead of the competition. Adaptable employees are also more likely to be able to take on new roles and responsibilities, which can lead to promotions and career advancement.

Adaptability also allows employees to be more flexible and open-minded, which can be a valuable asset in the workplace. For example, if an employee is adaptable, they may be more willing to take on new tasks or projects outside of their comfort zone, or to consider different approaches to problem-solving. This willingness to try new things and think creatively can make them more valuable to their organization and increase their chances of promotion.

In addition to the benefits for individual employees, adaptability can also have a positive impact on the organization as a whole. When employees are adaptable, they can help their organization respond more effectively to changes in the business environment. This can help the organization stay ahead of the competition, innovate, and grow. Moreover, adaptable employees can contribute to a positive and collaborative culture within the organization, as they are more open to new ideas and approaches.

There are several ways that employees can develop and enhance their adaptability skills. One approach is to seek out new challenges and learning opportunities, such as taking on new roles or responsibilities, or participating in professional development training. This can help employees expand their skills and knowledge, and become more adaptable. It is also important for employees to stay open-minded and receptive to new ideas, and to be willing to try new approaches or techniques.

Another way to develop adaptability is to embrace a growth mindset, which is the belief that skills and abilities can be developed and improved through effort and learning. This mindset can help employees embrace challenges and change, and be more open to learning and growth. It is also important for employees to be resilient, which is the ability to bounce back from setbacks and challenges. Resilient employees are more likely to adapt to change and stay motivated, even in difficult circumstances.

In conclusion, adaptability is a crucial skill that can significantly aid in career progression and promotion in the workplace. It enables employees to thrive in an increasingly dynamic and fast-paced business world, and to continuously learn and grow. It also allows employees to be more flexible and open-minded, which can be a valuable asset to their organization.

By seeking out new challenges and learning opportunities, embracing a growth mindset, and being resilient, employees can develop and enhance their adaptability skills and increase their chances of promotion.

SCENARIO...
As a young employee at a fast-growing startup, Sarah knew that she needed to stand out if she wanted to climb the corporate ladder. She had always been a hard worker, but she realized that there was more to success than just putting in long hours.

One day, Sarah overheard her boss talking about how important adaptability was for employees to succeed in the ever-changing world of business. She knew that she needed to develop this skill if she wanted to stand out from her coworkers and earn a promotion.

Sarah began by observing her colleagues and how they responded to change. She noticed that some people resisted change and became frustrated when things didn't go according to plan. Others were more open to new ideas and approaches, and seemed to thrive in a constantly evolving environment.

Sarah knew that she needed to be more like the latter group if she wanted to succeed. She started by asking her boss for more challenging assignments and taking on additional responsibilities outside of her job description. This not only helped her build her skills and knowledge, but it also showed her boss that she was willing to take on new challenges and adapt to change.

As Sarah gained more experience and proved her adaptability, she began to be noticed by higher-level executives.

She was offered more important projects and given the opportunity to work on cross-functional teams, which exposed her to a wide range of business areas and allowed her to learn from more experienced colleagues.

Eventually, Sarah's adaptability and willingness to take on new challenges paid off. She was offered a promotion to a leadership role, where she was able to use her skills to guide her team through the constant changes and challenges of the business world.

Sarah's story illustrates the importance of adaptability in the workplace. By being open to new ideas and approaches, and showing a willingness to take on new challenges, she was able to stand out and earn a promotion. This valuable skill will continue to serve her well as she grows in her career and takes on even greater responsibilities.

13. LEADERSHIP SKILL

Leadership skills are essential for success in the workplace. They are the qualities that enable individuals to inspire, motivate, and guide others toward a common goal. These skills are particularly important for those seeking promotion, as they demonstrate an ability to take on additional responsibilities and effectively lead a team. In this essay, we will explore how leadership skills can aid promotion in the workplace.

One of the key ways in which leadership skills can aid promotion is by demonstrating an ability to take charge and make decisions. In the modern business world, leaders are expected to be proactive and take initiative in driving projects forward. This means being able to identify problems and opportunities, and developing strategies to address them. Those who demonstrate an ability to make tough decisions, even in the face of uncertainty, are often viewed as strong leaders and are more likely to be promoted.

Another way in which leadership skills can aid promotion is by building strong relationships with colleagues. Successful leaders are able to build strong connections with their team members and create a positive work environment. This can be achieved through effective communication, listening to others, and being open and transparent. Strong relationships with colleagues can help to foster a sense of trust and respect, which is essential for any successful team.

Leadership skills also involve being able to inspire and motivate others. This means being able to set a clear vision and communicate it effectively to the team. It also involves being able to provide support and guidance to help team members achieve their goals. Those who are able to inspire and motivate their team are more likely to be viewed as strong leaders, and are therefore more likely to be considered for promotion.

In addition to these skills, successful leaders must also be able to adapt to change. This means being able to respond quickly and effectively to new challenges and opportunities, and being able to pivot when necessary. Those who are able to navigate change effectively are more likely to be viewed as strong leaders, and are therefore more likely to be considered for promotion.

Finally, leadership skills also involve being able to delegate effectively. This means being able to identify the strengths of each team member and assigning tasks accordingly. It also involves being able to trust others to complete tasks to the best of their ability and providing support as needed. Those who are able to delegate effectively are more likely to be viewed as strong leaders, and are therefore more likely to be considered for promotion.

In conclusion, leadership skills are essential for success in the workplace, and are particularly important for those seeking promotion. These skills include the ability to take charge and make decisions, build strong relationships with colleagues, inspire and motivate others, adapt to change, and delegate effectively. By demonstrating these skills, individuals are more likely to be viewed as strong leaders and are therefore more likely to be considered for promotion.

SCENARIO...
It was the last day of the week, and Serena was feeling overwhelmed as she sat at her desk, staring at her overflowing inbox. As a junior employee at a large corporation, she often found herself feeling like she was drowning in work and struggling to keep up with the demands of her job.

But despite the challenges, Serena was determined to succeed and make a name for herself within the company.

One day, as she was working late in the office, she overheard a conversation between her boss and a senior executive. They were discussing a promotion opportunity within the company and how to choose the best candidate for the role.

As Serena listened to their conversation, she realized that she had the skills and experience necessary to be considered for the promotion. But she knew that simply having the right qualifications wasn't enough - she needed to demonstrate strong leadership skills to stand out from the competition.

With this realization, Emily decided to take action and began working on developing her leadership skills. She started by seeking out opportunities to take on additional responsibilities and lead small projects within her team. She also made a conscious effort to be more proactive and take charge of situations, rather than waiting for others to lead the way.

As she applied these leadership skills in her daily work, Serena noticed a significant change in the way she was perceived by her colleagues and superiors. People started taking notice of her contributions and she was frequently praised for her strong work ethic and ability to lead others.

With each new project she tackled and each successful outcome, Serena's confidence grew. She became more assertive and began speaking up in meetings, offering her thoughts and ideas on how to solve problems and improve processes.

As the months went by, Serena's hard work and leadership skills began to pay off. She was offered the promotion she had been working towards and was thrilled to take on the new role.

Over the years, Serena continued to excel in her career, using her leadership skills to inspire and motivate her team. She became a valuable asset to the company and was eventually promoted to a senior leadership position.

Looking back on her journey, Serena realized that it was her dedication to developing her leadership skills that had helped her gain the promotion she had always wanted. She learned that with hard work, determination, and focus on improving oneself, anything is possible.

GOING UP?

END

www.ingramcontent.com/pod-product-compliance
Lightning Source LLC
Chambersburg PA
CBHW051536240526
45465CB00027B/434